POINTS OF VIEW

Should Schools Have DRESS CODES?

By Layla Owens

KidHaven PUBLISHING

Published in 2022 by
KidHaven Publishing, an Imprint of Greenhaven Publishing, LLC
353 3rd Avenue
Suite 255
New York, NY 10010

Designer: Deanna Paternostro
Editor: Kaite Kawa

Photo credits: Cover wavebreakmedia/Shutterstock.com; pp. 5 (left), 9 Klaus Vedfelt/DigitalVision/Getty Images; p. 5 (right) Sue Barr/Image Source/Getty Images; p. 7 Mohammed Huwais/Stringer/AFP/Getty Images; p. 11 The Washington Post/Contributor/The Washington Post/Getty Images; p. 13 monkeybusinessimages/iStock/Getty Images Plus/Getty Images; p. 15 Westend61/Getty Images; p. 17 DGLimages/iStock/Getty Images Plus/Getty Images; pp. 19, 21 (inset, right) SDI Productions/E+/Getty Images; p. 21 (notepad) ESB Professional/Shutterstock.com; p. 21 (markers) Kucher Serhii/Shutterstock.com; p. 21 (photo frame) FARBAI/iStock/Thinkstock; p. 21 (inset, left) Highwaystarz-Photography/iStock/Getty Images Plus/Getty Images; p. 21 (inset, middle left) Cavan Images/Cavan/Getty Images; p. 21 (inset, middle right) gpointstudio/iStock/Getty Images Plus/Getty Images.

Library of Congress Cataloging-in-Publication Data

Names: Owens, Layla, author.
Title: Should schools have dress codes? / Layla Owens.
Description: New York : KidHaven Publishing, [2022] | Series: Points of view | Includes bibliographical references and index.
Identifiers: LCCN 2020030749 | ISBN 9781534536432 (library binding) | ISBN 9781534536418 (paperback) | ISBN 9781534536425 (set) | ISBN 9781534536449 (ebook)
Subjects: LCSH: Dress codes–Juvenile literature. | School children's clothing. | Debates and debating–Juvenile literature.
Classification: LCC LB3024 .O94 2022 | DDC 371.8–dc23
LC record available at https://lccn.loc.gov/2020030749

Printed in the United States of America

CPSIA compliance information: Batch #CS22KH: For further information contact Greenhaven Publishing LLC, New York, New York at 1-844-317-7404.

Please visit our website, www.greenhavenpublishing.com. For a free color catalog of all our high-quality books, call toll free 1-844-317-7404 or fax 1-844-317-7405.

Find us on

CONTENTS

Cracking the Code	4
Dress Codes Around the World	6
Distractions and Discomfort	8
Discrimination	10
Beyond Bullying	12
Express Yourself!	14
Dress for Success	16
More Learning, Fewer Time-Outs	18
Dress Code Decisions	20
Glossary	22
For More Information	23
Index	24

Cracking the CODE

Do you wear a uniform to school, or can you wear whatever you'd like? Most schools fall somewhere in the middle. They have dress codes, which tell students what they can wear.

Some people think dress codes are necessary. They believe these codes keep kids safe from bullying. They can also help students pay attention to their schoolwork and not each other's outfits. Other people believe that dress codes keep students from **expressing** themselves. They believe students are **punished** unfairly for how they dress. Let's look at both sides of this heated **debate**!

Know the Facts!

Around 53 percent of public schools had a strict, or firm, dress code in the 2016–2017 school year.

People on both sides of the dress code debate have reasons for their opinions. If you look at both sides and study the facts, you can make an informed, or educated, decision about school dress codes.

Dress Codes Around THE WORLD

You might think dress codes apply only to schools. However, dress codes have been around since ancient Greece! Sometimes entire countries have dress codes, even today.

In Saudi Arabia, Muslim women must cover their bodies. They often wear long black cloaks called abayas and head and face coverings called niqabs. Other countries, such as France, have laws against covering one's face in public. In these countries, niqabs are banned, or not allowed. Some dress codes are based on **modesty**, and others are based on safety.

Know the Facts!

Dress codes are often different for women and men.

In some countries, it's part of the dress code for girls to wear head coverings in public.

Distractions and DISCOMFORT

Some people argue that dress codes and uniforms are helpful because they get rid of **distractions**. Students go to school to learn, so anything that distracts them from learning doesn't belong in a school setting. Bad words on clothing, flashy clothing, or clothing that shows too much skin could make it hard for others to pay attention in school.

People also say that certain clothes can make other people feel uncomfortable. For example, T-shirts with **racist** language could be hurtful to students from **minority** groups. Shirts with rude sayings about women could also make people feel uncomfortable.

Know the Facts!

Some Americans wear the Confederate flag on their clothing. It stands for the side in the American Civil War (1861–1865) that supported slavery, so this clothing makes some people uncomfortable.

Some people say that uniforms and dress codes make it easier for kids to learn.

DISCRIMINATION

People who oppose dress codes say they can lead to discrimination. Discrimination is treating someone unfairly based on differences like race, age, or sex. Dress codes sometimes call out hair and clothing styles often worn by minority groups. Those students may be unfairly punished for not following rules.

Many dress codes, such as those with rules about the length of shorts and skirts, discriminate against girls. People sometimes say this clothing is distracting for other students, especially boys. Others argue that the wearer shouldn't be punished for how people see them. It's important to know that there are laws against discrimination.

Know the Facts!

A 2018 study by the National Women's Law Center found that dress code punishments can cause Black female students to fall behind in school.

Some girls have spoken out against dress codes, saying that female students shouldn't be punished for others' distraction.

Beyond BULLYING

Some people think that dress codes help stop bullying. Students whose families have a lot of money might set a high bar for fashion in their school. That could lead them to bully those who have less money and can't buy popular clothes. Students might also bully others for wearing clothes that are different or show more skin.

People who believe in dress codes think that they help even the playing field of school fashion. If everyone has to follow the same rules, they feel, students are more equal. Then, bullies have one less thing to tease someone about.

Know the Facts!

A 2019 study from the National Center for Educational Statistics found that 1 in 5 students reported being bullied.

Some people think dress codes make kids feel more equal. This can help stop certain kinds of bullying.

Express YOURSELF!

Some people think that clothing helps people express themselves as individuals. You might feel more like you when you wear glitter or bright colors. You might feel most comfortable in baggy clothes and sporty shoes. You might feel **confident** when you wear a shirt with your favorite animal or sports team on it. Feeling comfortable and confident can help students have a better time in school.

Some people think allowing students to choose their own clothes makes them more independent. It can also make them more creative and able to think in new ways.

Know the Facts!

Researchers—people who study a subject closely—have found that creativity in kids has declined, or gone down, greatly in the last three decades.

What kind of clothing makes you feel most creative or comfortable?

Dress for SUCCESS

Many jobs have some sort of dress code. Because of that, some people think that dress codes help students dress for success.

If school is practice for a job, then dressing the part may help kids work toward that goal. They may learn how to follow rules and directions. Dress codes might help put students in the right mindset to do schoolwork. Dressing under dress code rules or in a uniform can also cut down on the amount of time it takes to decide on an outfit each day. That can help kids be on time for school.

Know the Facts!

Almost 20 percent of public schools require their students to wear uniforms.

Some schools think dress codes help students stay on task.

More Learning, Fewer TIME-OUTS

While some people argue that not having a dress code can take away from learning, others think the opposite. They believe punishing kids for going against a dress code can take away from their learning even more.

Imagine that a student is turned away from class every time they wear something that doesn't meet the dress code. They might spend time at the principal's office or be **suspended** from school. "Dress coding" punishments can make a student miss important lessons and schoolwork. Then they may fall behind in class. Since dress codes often target girls and people in minority groups more, this makes them more likely to fall behind than white boys.

Know the Facts!

A 2018 study by the National Women's Law Center found that 3 out of 4 public high school dress codes allowed students to be pulled from class because of their clothing.

Time out of class for "dress coding" can be harmful to students who want to learn, regardless of what they wear.

Dress Code DECISIONS

You've heard both sides of the dress code debate. You can use the opinions of others, the facts, and your own experience, or life events, to decide what you think.

Are dress codes setting kids up for success, or is it more important to be able to express your creativity than to be like everyone else? Public and private schools in different areas often have different ideas about how students should dress. That doesn't mean things can't change, though. You can have an informed talk with people about this important topic now that you have the facts!

Know the Facts!

How do adults feel about dress codes at work? One study found that 1 in 3 workers would rather dress **casually** than have a $5,000 increase in pay per year.

Should schools have dress codes?

YES

- Some clothing causes students to be distracted and uncomfortable and takes away from learning.
- Dress codes decrease bullying.
- Dress codes help kids "dress for success."

NO

- Dress codes can discriminate against women and people in minority groups.
- Kids should be able to express themselves through clothing to encourage creativity and independence.
- "Dress coding" punishments take students away from schoolwork.

There are many arguments for and against dress codes. Which ones do you agree with?

GLOSSARY

casual: Designed for informal use.

confident: Having a feeling of belief that you can do something well.

debate: An argument or discussion about an issue, generally between two sides. Also, to take part in such an argument or discussion.

distraction: Something that draws a person's thoughts or attention away from something else.

express: To make thoughts and feelings known.

minority: A group of people who are different from the larger group in a country or other area in some way, such as race or religion.

modesty: The quality of behaving and dressing in ways that do not attract attention.

punish: To make someone suffer for doing something wrong.

racist: Describing the practice of treating others poorly because they are part of a different race, or group of people who look alike in certain ways.

suspend: To keep a student out of school.

For More INFORMATION

WEBSITES

Are School Dress Codes Fair?
choices.scholastic.com/issues/2018-19/020119/are-school-dress-codes-fair.html
Read the arguments of students who are for and against dress codes.

Dealing with Bullies
kidshealth.org/en/kids/bullies.html
Some dress codes are meant to protect against bullying. Explore this website for more suggestions for how to deal with bullies.

BOOKS

Adamson, Heather. *Clothes in Many Cultures*. Oxford, UK: Raintree Publishers, 2018.

Lacey, Jane, and Venitia Dean. *Dealing with Bullying*. New York, NY: PowerKids Press, 2019.

Sotomayor, Sonia. *Just Ask! Be Different, Be Brave, Be You*. New York, NY: Philomel Books, 2019.

INDEX

B

bullying, 4, 12, 13

C

creativity, 14, 20, 21

D

discrimination, 10, 11

distractions, 8, 9, 10, 21

F

France, 6

G

Greece, 6

H

hair, 10

J

jobs, 16

L

laws, 6

M

men and boys, 6, 10, 18

minority groups, 8, 10, 18, 21

P

private schools, 20

public schools, 4, 16, 18, 20

R

racist language, 8

S

Saudi Arabia, 6

schoolwork, 4, 16, 18, 21

U

uniform, 4, 8, 9, 16

W

women and girls, 6, 7, 8, 10, 11, 18, 21